The Question & Answer Book

WORLD OF WEATHER

WORLD OF WEATHER

By David Adler
Illustrated by Ray Burns

Troll Associates

Library of Congress Cataloging in Publication Data

Adler, David A.
    World of weather.

    (The Question and answer book)
    Summary: Questions and answers provide basic informa-
tion about weather, including the formation of winds,
snow, and thunderstorms.
    1. Weather—Juvenile literature. [1. Weather.
2. Questions and answers] I. Burns, Raymond, 1924-
ill. II. Title. III. Series.
QC863.5.A34   1983   551.6   82-17398
ISBN 0-89375-870-1
ISBN 0-89375-871-X (pbk.)

86 - 320

Printed in the United States of America
10   9   8   7   6   5   4   3   2   1

What is weather?

Weather is the condition of the air outside. Just step outside and you can tell what the weather is today. You will also get a few hints about what makes the weather. Is the sun shining? Is the air calm, or is it windy? Does the air feel damp and wet? Is it raining? It is the sun, air, and water—acting together—which give us our weather.

5

How does the sun affect the weather?

The sun gives us heat. The longer the sun is out during the day, the more heat we get—and the higher the temperature is. In summer, the sun rises earlier and sets later than it does in winter. Wherever it is summer, the Earth receives more sunlight than it does in other seasons. The Earth stores the sun's heat and warms the air around it. In winter, there are fewer hours of sunlight. One reason the summer is warmer than winter is that in summer there are more hours of sunlight.

Another reason summer is warmer than winter is that summer sunlight is warmer than winter sunlight. That's because the summer sun shines directly above us. In the winter, the sunlight comes to us at a more slanted angle.

When it's hot outside, it's because the sun has heated the Earth. The Earth stores heat from the sun and warms the surrounding air. You can actually feel the Earth storing heat from the sun.

Try this experiment.

Fill a paper plate with dry garden soil. The soil should be taken from a cool, shaded place. Put it in the sunlight and wait a few minutes. Then touch the soil. Is it warm? Wait a few more minutes and touch the soil again. Is it warmer? The longer you leave the soil in the sunlight, the warmer it will become. The soil is storing up heat from the sun.

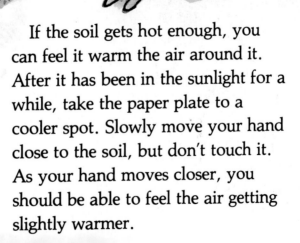

If the soil gets hot enough, you can feel it warm the air around it. After it has been in the sunlight for a while, take the paper plate to a cooler spot. Slowly move your hand close to the soil, but don't touch it. As your hand moves closer, you should be able to feel the air getting slightly warmer.

What makes the wind?

The sun gives us heat. The sun *and* the air together give us *wind*. This is how it happens. First, the sun heats the Earth. The Earth then heats the air, and the warm air rises. Cool air quickly moves in to take its place. Then this cool air is warmed, and it rises, too. More cool air rushes in. This moving air is called wind.

Where does all this cool air come from?

On a summer day, it could be air that comes from above an ocean, a river, or a lake. The air above water stays cooler than the air above land because water does not heat up as quickly as land. In summer, this cooler air blows toward land to replace the rising warm air.

The air is also cooler in places that get little sunlight—under trees, on the shady side of a mountain, and toward the North and South Poles. This cool air is constantly moving in to replace the rising warm air.

If you go outside and hold up a flag or a light piece of cloth, you can tell how quickly the air is moving. If the air is calm, the flag will hang down limply. If the air is moving, the flag will move, too. In a strong wind, the flag will stretch straight out.

Winds can be dangerous.

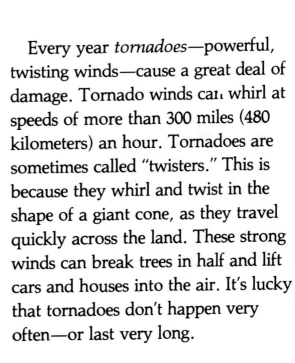

Every year *tornadoes*—powerful, twisting winds—cause a great deal of damage. Tornado winds can whirl at speeds of more than 300 miles (480 kilometers) an hour. Tornadoes are sometimes called "twisters." This is because they whirl and twist in the shape of a giant cone, as they travel quickly across the land. These strong winds can break trees in half and lift cars and houses into the air. It's lucky that tornadoes don't happen very often—or last very long.

Hurricane winds are also very powerful and dangerous. These winds, which begin in the air over the ocean, blow at more than 74 miles (118 kilometers) an hour. Hurricane winds sweep over a much larger area than tornadoes, and they also last much longer. Hurricanes can cause a great amount of damage, destroying homes, sinking ships, and causing floods.

Along with the strong winds of a hurricane come heavy, drenching rains. Many tons of water may fall during these heavy downpours.

How do rain clouds form?

Rain is a kind of *precipitation*—moisture that falls to the Earth. Rain and other kinds of precipitation—sleet, snow, and hail—fall from clouds. You've seen clouds floating in the sky. Would you like to know how clouds are formed? Try this simple experiment.

15

Put a little water in a bowl. Leave the bowl out in the sun. After a few hours, what happens to the water in the bowl? If you leave the bowl in the sun long enough, the water will disappear. It will have *evaporated*—turned into an invisible gas called *water vapor*. Water vapor is moisture in the air that you cannot see. When there is a lot of moisture in the air, we say the weather is humid. The air is muggy when it is warm and humid at the same time.

After the water in your bowl evaporates, there will be water vapor floating in the air. Rising warm air carries the invisible moisture high up in the sky. The air high up in the sky is cool. This cool air changes the vapor back into tiny droplets of water. Billions of tiny droplets of water gathered together make a cloud.

17

Of course the water from one small bowl is not enough to make a cloud. The water in puddles, pools, rivers, lakes, and oceans also evaporates and helps form clouds. Fortunately, large lakes and oceans don't completely evaporate. That's because the clouds they help to form cause rain. The rain falls back into the lakes and oceans and keeps them full.

What is the inside of a cloud like?

From the outside, a cloud looks like a big puff of floating white smoke. But what is the *inside* of a cloud like? If you've ever walked through fog, you know what the inside of a cloud is like. Fog is really a cloud that is resting on the ground.

After you walk through fog, you may feel a little damp. That's because fog and clouds are made up of billions of tiny droplets of water floating in the air. When you walk through fog, you are really walking through floating water—and some of it comes off on your skin and clothes.

In a cloud, those droplets of water are always moving. They bump into each other, stick together, and collect into larger drops of water. When the drops become too large and heavy to be held up in the air, they fall to the ground as rain.

The water in clouds does not *always* fall as rain. Sometimes rain falls through very cold air. On the way down to Earth, the raindrops freeze into bits of ice called *sleet*. Sleet is really frozen rain.

How is snow formed?

Open the freezer of your refrigerator and look inside. Has *frost*—a white powdery kind of ice—formed over some of the frozen food? That frost was formed in much the way snow is formed in a cloud.

The air in your refrigerator contains water vapor. Frost is frozen water vapor. Sometimes the air inside a cloud is so cold that the vapor freezes into snow.

Snow can be very beautiful when it covers the land. Each tiny snowflake is also beautiful. The next time it snows, catch a snowflake on your sleeve or on a dark piece of paper. Look at it through a magnifying glass. You will see that it has six sides. Every snowflake has six sides—yet all snowflakes are different. No matter how many you catch and look at, you will never find two exactly alike!

Have you ever been hit by a hailstone?

It hurts. *Hailstones* are balls of ice
that fall from clouds. Most hailstones
are small—about the size of a pea.
But some hailstones are as big as
baseballs.

If you cut a hailstone in half, you
will see how hailstones are formed.
Inside you will find that the hailstone
is made up of layers of ice. The
larger the hailstone, the more layers
you'll find.

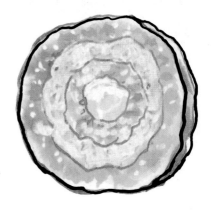

Hailstones are formed during thunderstorms. These balls of ice begin to form high in the cold, upper part of a cloud. The layers of the hailstone form as the hailstone falls through the cloud toward the ground, picking up more freezing moisture as it travels.

Each time water freezes around a hailstone, a layer of ice is formed. As more layers of ice form, the hailstones get larger and heavier. When the hailstones are too heavy to be held up by the wind, they fall to the ground. Large hailstones can break windows, dent cars, and kill plants. During a hailstorm, it's a good idea to stay inside.

It's also a good idea to stay inside during a thunderstorm. The *lightning* you see during a thunderstorm is a huge spark of electricity that jumps from cloud to cloud, or that jumps from a cloud to the Earth. All that electricity can be dangerous.

What causes lightning?

Inside a cloud, warm air is rising and cool air is sinking down to take its place. Tiny drops of water are moving, too. These drops of water rub against each other. Huge charges of electricity are built up. Then—CRASH! You see lightning—a big spark of electricity jumping from a cloud to the Earth. A few seconds later—BOOM! You hear thunder —the sound lightning causes. You hear the thunder *after* you see the lightning because sound travels through the air more slowly than the light from the flash of lightning.

The next time you see lightning, start counting.

Count the seconds that pass from
the time you see the lightning until
you hear the thunder. The number
of seconds that pass will tell you
how far away the lightning struck.
The lightning is one mile away from
you for every five seconds you count.

Can you forecast the weather?

You know that weather is the condition of the air outside. You know the sun, air, and water acting together make the weather. You know what the weather was like yesterday. But can you tell what the weather will be like later today? Will it be sunny? Should you plan to go swimming, or will rain force you to stay indoors?

You can look up at the clouds to find out what the weather will probably be like. Clouds are not all the same. Some clouds look big and white and puffy—like large floating cotton balls. These are *cumulus* clouds. When you see them, it means the weather will be clear. Cumulus clouds are fair-weather clouds.

Cirrus clouds look thin and light and wispy—like feathers floating in the sky. When you see them, the weather will probably change.

When you see clouds that are low, straight, and that stretch across the sky in flat layers, get your umbrella. Those are *stratus* clouds. When you see them, you know it will probably rain.

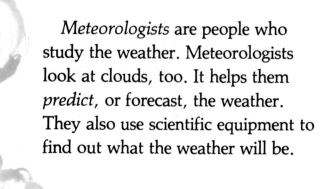

Meteorologists are people who study the weather. Meteorologists look at clouds, too. It helps them *predict*, or forecast, the weather. They also use scientific equipment to find out what the weather will be.

When you're sick, you may use a thermometer to measure your temperature. Meteorologists use thermometers to measure the temperature of the air.

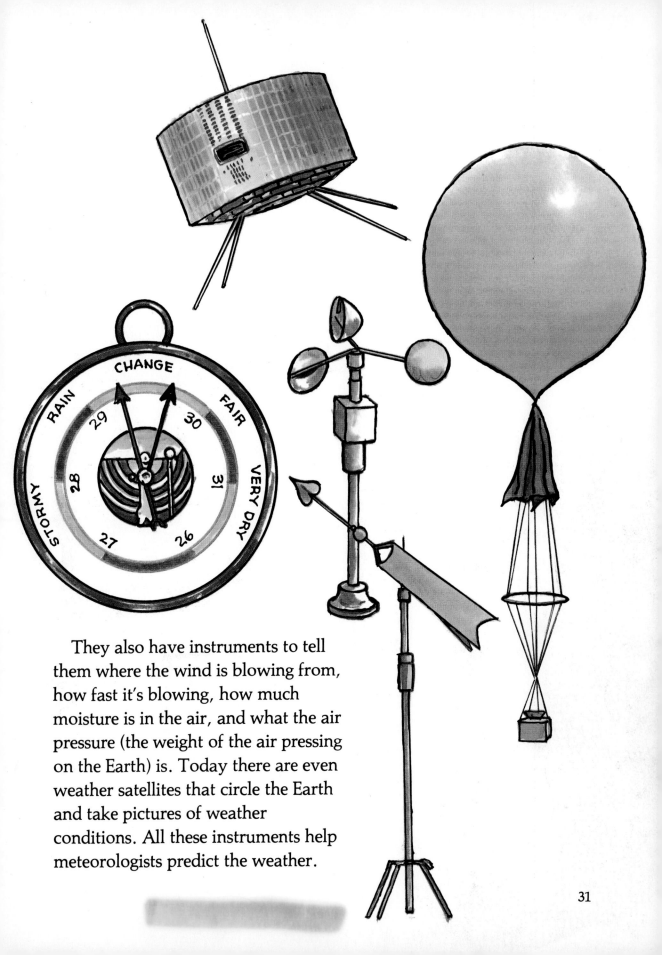

They also have instruments to tell them where the wind is blowing from, how fast it's blowing, how much moisture is in the air, and what the air pressure (the weight of the air pressing on the Earth) is. Today there are even weather satellites that circle the Earth and take pictures of weather conditions. All these instruments help meteorologists predict the weather.

Can we control the weather?

We know that the sun, air, and water together make our weather. Today we are able to predict what the weather will be. Wouldn't it be wonderful if we could make the sun shine whenever we wanted—or make it snow or rain? People have been trying to control the weather for hundreds of years. But they haven't succeeded very well.

Although we can't control it, the weather affects every one of us. Whether it is sunny, cloudy, rainy, snowy, hot, or cold, the weather is an important and interesting part of our planet Earth.

Date Due

D.Att					
Gordan					
Gxeel					
JAN 2 1 1992					
APR 2 8 1992					
Mutch					
Queensland					
MacArthur					